PIANO SOLO

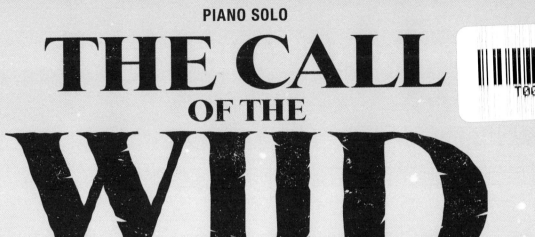

THE CALL OF THE WILD

MUSIC FROM THE MOTION PICTURE SOUNDTRACK
MUSIC BY JOHN POWELL

Piano Solo Arrangements by Batu Sener

ISBN 978-1-5400-9252-6

Visit Hal Leonard Online at
www.halleonard.com

Contact us:
Hal Leonard
7777 West Bluemound Road
Milwaukee, WI 53213
Email: info@halleonard.com

In Europe, contact:
Hal Leonard Europe Limited
42 Wigmore Street
Marylebone, London, W1U 2RN
Email: info@halleonardeurope.com

In Australia, contact:
Hal Leonard Australia Pty. Ltd.
4 Lentara Court
Cheltenham, Victoria, 3192 Australia
Email: info@halleonard.com.au

WAKE THE GIRLS

Music by JOHN POWELL

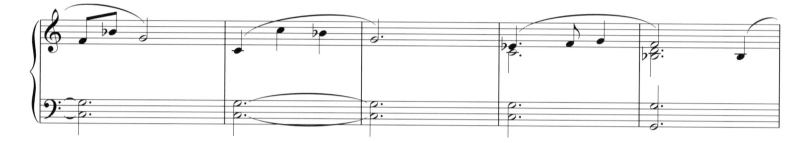

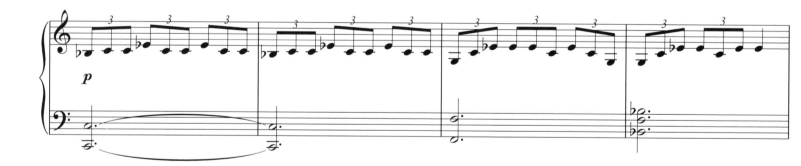

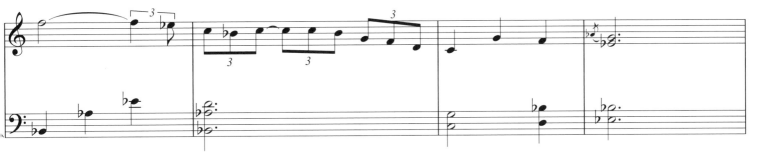

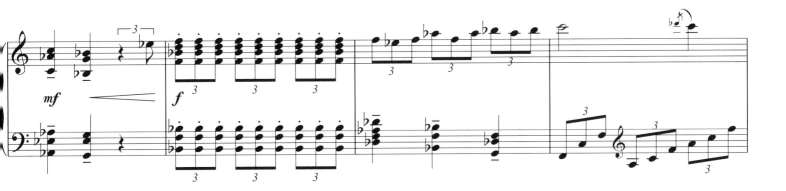

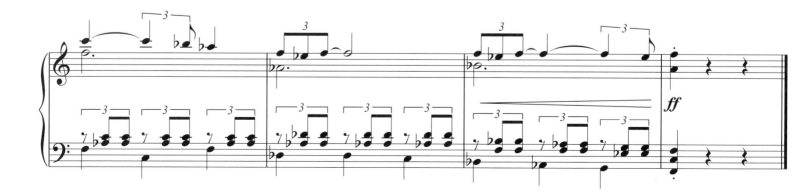

JOINING THE TEAM

Music by JOHN POWELL

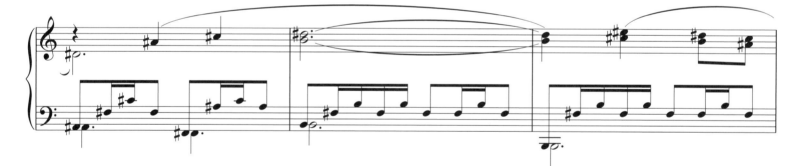

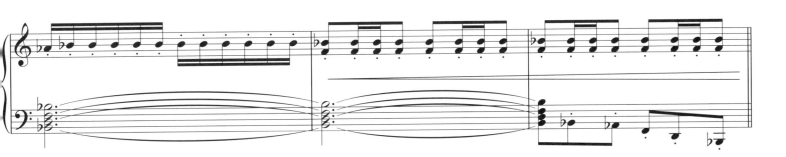

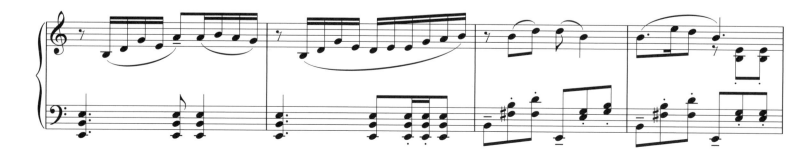

SNOWY CLIMB

Music by JOHN POWELL

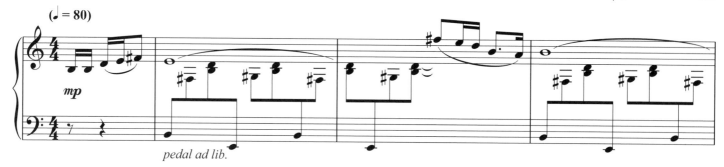

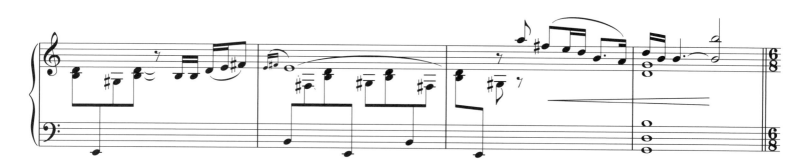

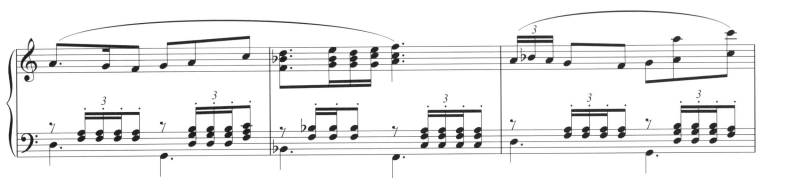

BUCK TAKES THE LEAD

Music by JOHN POWELL

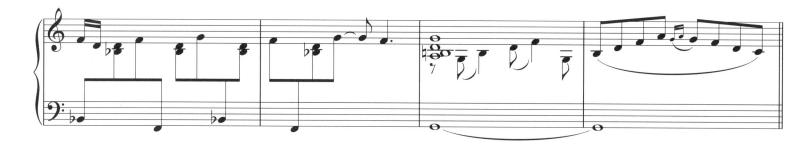

(♩ = 94)

cresc.

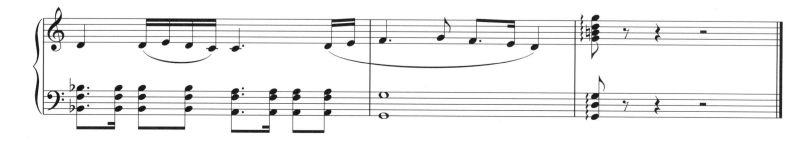

NEWFANGLED TELEGRAM

Music by JOHN POWELL

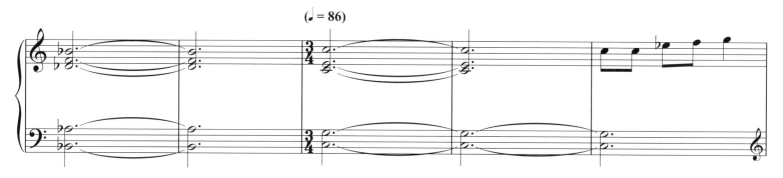

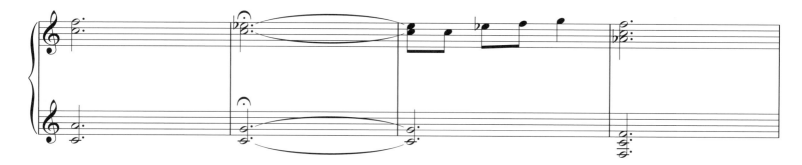

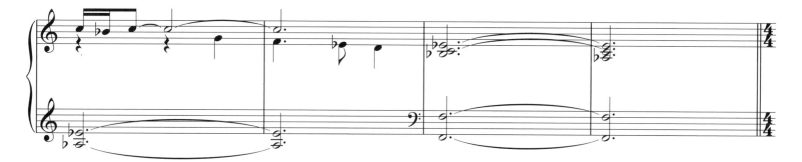

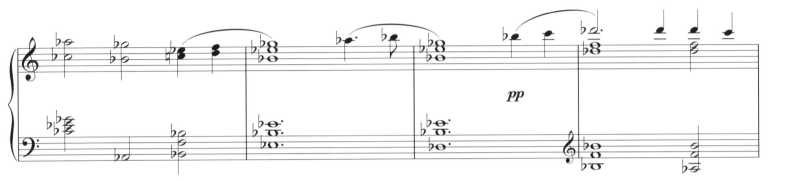

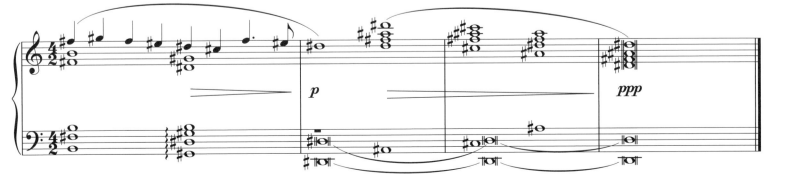

WE CARRY LOVE

Music by JOHN POWELL

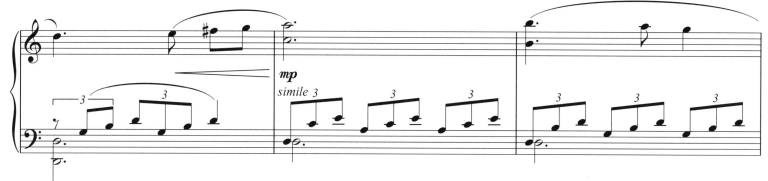

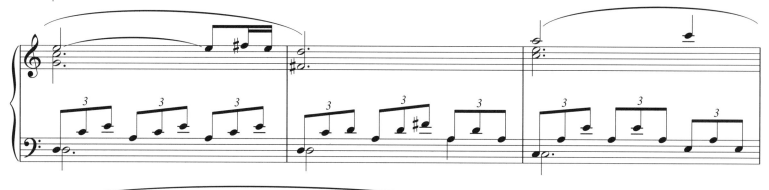

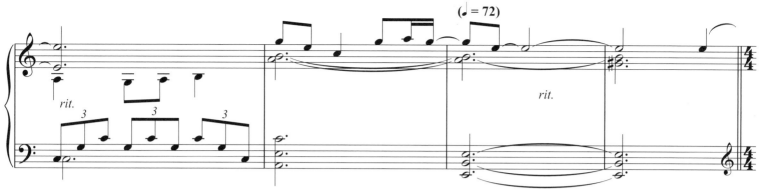

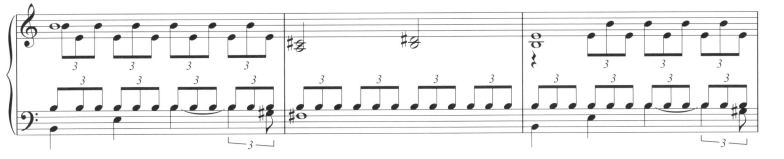

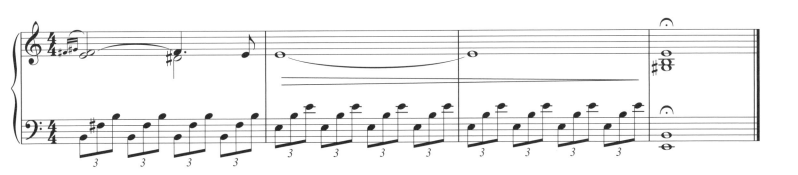

COULDN'T FIND THE WORDS

Music by JOHN POWELL

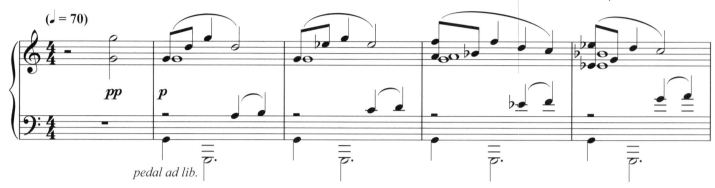

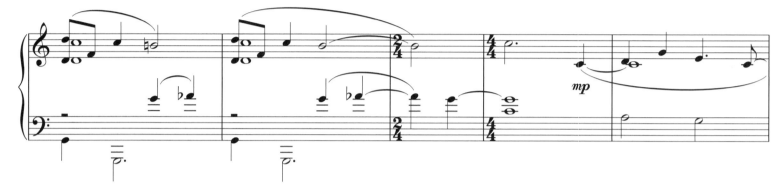

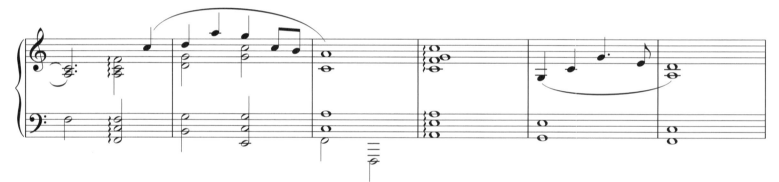

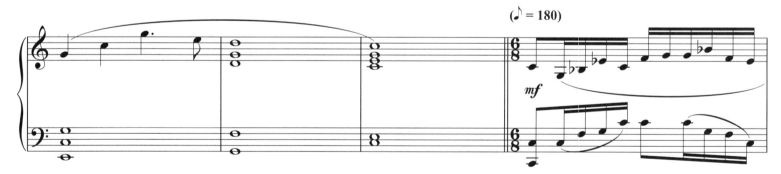

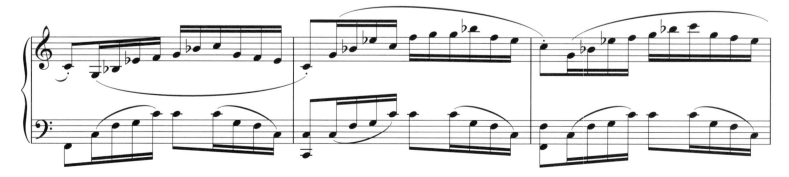

THEY'RE ALL GONE

Music by JOHN POWELL

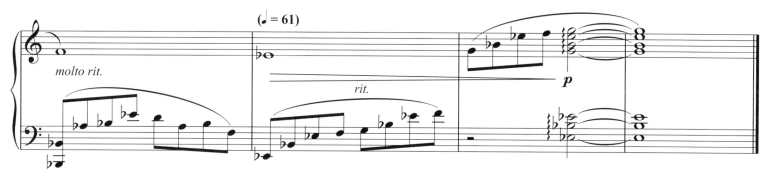

WHAT AN ADVENTURE

Music by JOHN POWELL

28

rit.

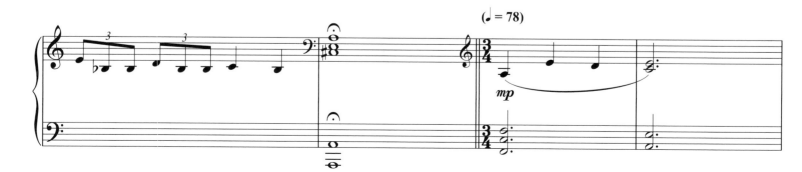

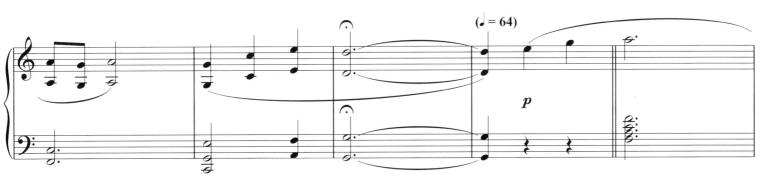

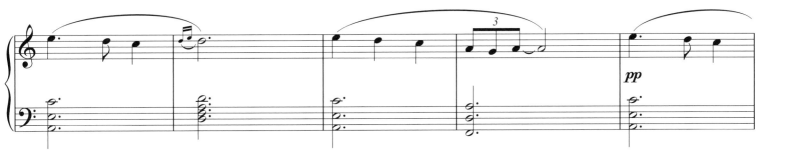

THE CALL OF THE WILD

Music by JOHN POWELL

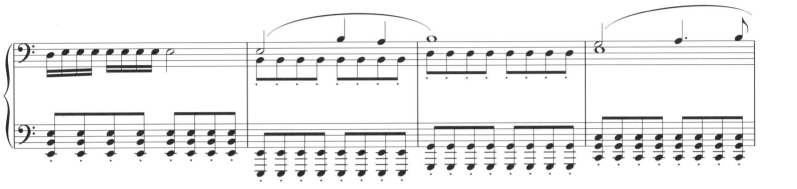

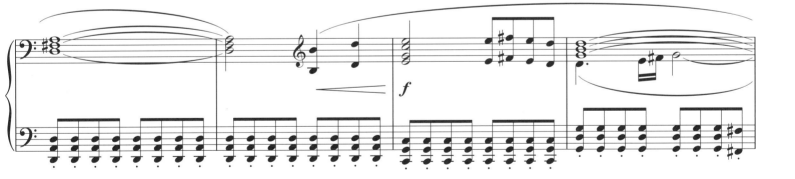

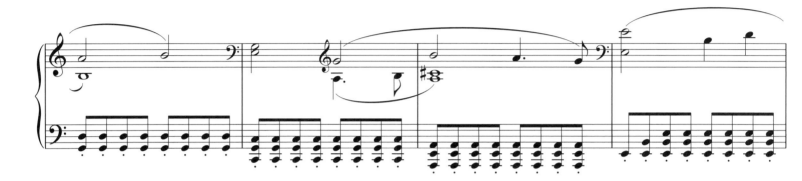

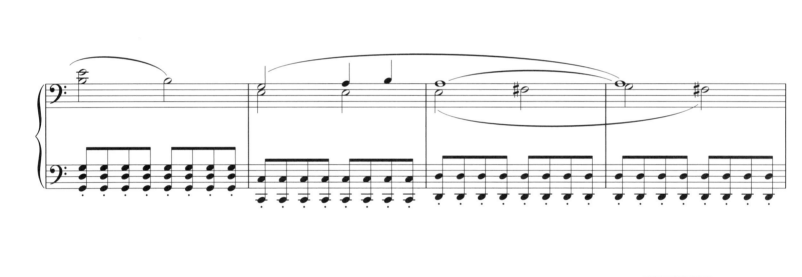

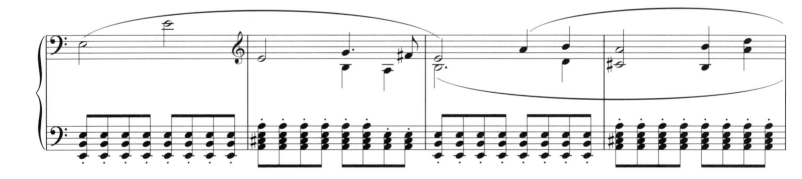

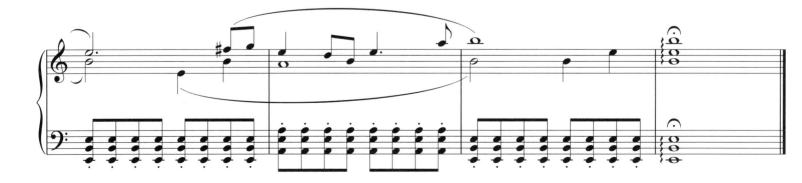